A GATEWAY TO WISDOM

PARADIGM SHIFT THINKING

JAMES A. JENKO

*Dedicated to my wife Crystal
and my son Ethan. Thank you
for the inspiration.*

TABLE OF CONTENTS

Preface 7

Introduction 11

Chapter 1 Ordinary Men 15

Chapter 2 Philosophy as a Way of Life 27

Chapter 3 Wisdom Over Intelligence 53

Chapter 4 Dialectic Over Debate 67

Chapter 5 What Is Really on the Line 91

Conclusion 100

Further Quotations for Contemplation 103

"Mankind so rarely produces a good book, one which with bold freedom sounds the battle-cry of truth, the song of philosophic heroism."

~ Nietzsche, *Philosophy in the Tragic Age of the Greeks*

PREFACE

Do not let the brevity of this book avert you from its depth. Our culture has become so shallow, let's learn to swim to great depths once again! The opening quote by Nietzsche serves as my aim in writing this book. Although a bold and high standard to try to live up to, even if I may have fallen a bit short of that ultimate aim, I believe the following content is of extreme value to all men at a time when the lessons within are desperately needed.

At a young age I came across a book about Socrates. I don't remember exactly which it was at this point, but that book had an impact on me, in that I realized that there were different and deeper ways of thinking and communicating about the issues of the world than I was typically being exposed to, even in a university environment. This created a sense of *wonder* that eventually inspired me to begin on a path of *seeking wisdom*. This ongoing journey has been consistently challenging, but just as equally rewarding. Throughout this ongoing journey I have found meaning, connection and inner peace, as well as many other valuable gifts that philosophy has to offer.

This is also very much the aim of this book for its readers—the beginning of a journey and to reveal that there are deeper, different, and better ways of thinking and communicating about all of the issues that we may find meaningful in our lives—specifically, different, deeper, and better than the typical cultural status quo. Although I am writing this at a specific point in time, the ideas throughout this book have been discussed by some of the greatest thinkers throughout history for thousands of years and have always been relevant and are just as relevant today.

Most of us realize the importance of trying to surround ourselves with good people—people who are honest, courageous, authentic and thoughtful. We can understand the benefit of being around people who are good examples, those who make us better men and women just by being in their presence and having the opportunity to learn from them.

Unfortunately, this is especially the case at a younger age when we may have less control over our environment, but even as we get older, it can be difficult to surround ourselves with great people all of the time— and it is impossible to surround ourselves with all of the greatest men throughout history. But one thing that I learned from a young age is that almost all of us can surround ourselves with *great books* by the greatest thinkers and doers throughout history. At a time when our current culture seems to be placing less and less value on dedicating the time to actually reading great books, I propose we need a *paradigm shift in thinking*. We need to reignite a love for reading and studying great philosophical thinkers. We desperately need to *reignite a love of wisdom*—the main role of philosophy. We need a paradigm shift in how we think and communicate with each other about the most important issues that impact all of our lives. I hope that this book can be the spark that reignites a love for wisdom and that serves as the impetus for a much-needed paradigm shift.

In the spirit of Socrates—"*I cannot teach anybody anything, I can only make them think*" and "*Wisdom begins in wonder*"—this book was written with similar sentiments and is intended to manifest a sense of *wonder* in the reader as the impetus to a philosophical *way of life* of self-transformation and seeking wisdom that can be of great benefit to the reader and subsequently their family and friends and society.

> **"There is no action of man in this life that is not the beginning of so long a chain of consequences as no human providence is high enough to give a man a prospect to the end."**
>
> ~ Thomas Hobbes, *Leviathan*

INTRODUCTION

A foolish man may pick up the Bible and become an even lesser man.

A wise man will pick up the Bible and become a better man.

An evil man can pick up the Bible and use it to manipulate and spread hatred and tyranny.

A righteous man can pick up the Bible and use it to spread goodness, truth, and beauty.

I propose that philosophy is the most important subject, because it is the subject that shapes the way we approach and think about every other subject. Philosophy is the first principle and we neglect it at our peril.

For example, many religious people may take that statement as blasphemy, countering that their religion is the most important subject, so I want to be clear that I am in no way diminishing the importance of anyone's religion or spirituality. Philosophy doesn't threaten religion or any other subject, but rather serves it—providing the intellectual tools and developing the character necessary to live out religious commitments thoughtfully and consistently. Even the most devout believer is engaged in philosophical work whenever they try to understand what their faith means and how it should shape their actions.

Think about this claim for a moment. Every decision you make, every belief you hold, every value you cherish operates from some philosophical foundation—whether you're conscious of it or not. When a scientist designs an experiment, they're operating from philosophical assumptions, such as "It is good to seek the truth." When parents discipline their children, they're acting from philosophical beliefs about human nature, moral development, and what constitutes flourishing. When business leaders make ethical decisions, they may be drawing from philosophical frameworks about justice, responsibility, and the good life. When business owners, plumbers, carpenters, and others interact with employees, customers, or coworkers they are making decisions about the proper way to treat people. When religious people interpret scripture and apply it to their daily life, they're engaging in philosophical reasoning about the relationship between eternal principles and temporal circumstances.

Consider a Christian wrestling with Jesus's teaching to "turn the other cheek"—does this mean complete pacifism in all situations? Should this teaching guide how a parent disciplines a child, how a police officer protects innocent people, or how a nation defends itself? These questions cannot be answered by simply reading the text—they require the same careful philosophical thinking that any complex moral question demands:

examining assumptions, considering counterarguments, weighing different interpretations, and seeking consistency between beliefs and actions. This is one role of philosophy—and one reason why philosophy was once considered one of the four pillars of knowledge.

Without proper philosophical training, most people have never deeply—or even moderately—examined these foundational assumptions and this can lead to self-deception and self-destructive actions, regardless of intentions. This is what I mean when I say *Philosophy is the first principle and we neglect it at our peril*. Therefore, this is a philosophy book intended for "ordinary men."

It's also important that I make clear from the beginning that just because this is a book for "ordinary men" that does not mean that I am going to dumb down the material, making it easier to read by sacrificing profundity or depth of the subject matter. This book is meant to challenge and lift people up rather than dumb the subject matter down. If there are words or concepts that are outside of your current vocabulary and understanding, it is your responsibility to investigate them further on your own. It is meant to be challenging while also being accessible.

Like any physical challenges one may take on, you have to start somewhere by challenging yourself. Intellectual exercise is no different. If you can only read and stay focused on a few sentences at a time, then that's how you start. It's analogous to only being able to run a short distance the first time to try to see how far you can run, but with training over time you can increase your ability to run longer distances. Similarly, you must keep training your mental focus and improving your reading comprehension and vocabulary in order for it to gradually improve.

This is a relatively short book, but it is one that should be read multiple times. There is some strategic repetition of ideas and quotes throughout as reminders and for emphasis. Specific excerpts that are italicized, bold, enlarged or some combination throughout carry very deep meaning and should be revisited often and contemplated deeply, not rushed or skimmed over. Each time you revisit this book you are likely to take some new and valuable insight away from it. Furthermore, at the end of each chapter I will provide a list of relevant resources to begin further investigation into the topics if you have begun to develop a sense of wonder.

CHAPTER 1

ORDINARY MEN

"The simple act of an ordinary brave man is not to participate in lies, not to support false actions! His rule: Let that come into the world, let it even reign supreme only NOT through me."

~ Aleksandr Solzhenitsyn

"That is why I have reiterated again and again that philosophy, unlike the investigative sciences, historical research, or mathematics, is everybody's business. All the latter are fields that tend toward greater and greater specialization and become the province of a wide variety of specialist experts. Philosophy alone, because of its intimate connection with the common-sense knowledge of the ordinary individual, remains unspecialized—the province of the generalist, the business of everybody."

~ Mortimer Adler, *Ten Philosophical Mistakes*

I will be clear about what I mean and what I do not mean when I use the word "ordinary" in this context. What I do not mean is to use the word as being synonymous with mediocrity. What I do mean to do is highlight the fact that "ordinary" is a precursor to "becoming extraordinary," as is needed in our own individual, unique lives and set of circumstances. Every extraordinary person was once ordinary. Every hero was once just another person facing challenges. Every individual who has developed a bit of wisdom was once ignorant and confused. What makes those that develop the capacity to become extraordinary is not some special gift or talent that only a few possess. The difference is a decision—a *philosophical* decision—a decision to take responsibility for one's own development, to refuse to accept limitations as permanent, to commit to the lifelong work of study and self-transformation.

PARADIGM SHIFT THINKING—WE MUST VALUE THE ACQUISITION OF AND PASSING ALONG OF KNOWLEDGE AND WISDOM OVER THE SUPERFICIAL COLLECTION OF MONEY AND STUFF.

The Jolly Tailor Who Became King

To give a few brief examples of what I'm talking about when I say "ordinary men," I'll start with a Polish folktale, "The Jolly Tailor Who Became King." As clinical psychologist Jordan Peterson summarizes in his book *Maps of Meaning*, the tale depicts an ordinary tailor who is called upon to sew up a dangerous hole in the sky to save the community. In the end, he voluntarily takes a great risk, saves the community, and becomes the hero: "The tailor—he who clothes, mends and ties—is the hero. Although simple (poor in outward appearance, humble, willing to take risks, helpful and kind), he has the capacity to become King."

This folktale encodes a profound truth: heroism is not the province of the naturally gifted or the obviously extraordinary. The tailor is chosen not because he is the strongest or the smartest or the most talented, but because he has developed the *character* qualities that make heroic action possible. He is wise enough to recognize the magnitude of the problem and that he has the skills that may be able to help. He has the courage and righteousness necessary to take great risks when appropriate.

Notice that his profession—tailoring—is fundamentally about repair and restoration. He mends what is torn, he creates order from chaos, and he takes disparate pieces then fashions them into something useful and beautiful. These are precisely the skills needed to address the existential problem that he faces. His ordinary work has been preparing him for extraordinary service all along. This is often how it works in real life as well. The person who has learned to be reliable in small things develops the character to be trustworthy in large things. The person who has practiced honesty and courage in everyday interactions develops the integrity and courageousness needed to speak truth in crucial moments. The person who has cultivated wisdom in ordinary decisions develops the prudence needed to navigate extraordinary challenges.

The Sword-Saint of Japan

For my next example, I turn to Miyamoto Musashi. Musashi was a philosopher and reputed to have been the greatest Japanese swordsman who ever lived. I specify *swordsman* because he did not have formal training from any one particular master to be considered a samurai. He was mostly self-taught and developed his own unique style using one short sword and one long sword simultaneously. He has been called the *Kensei*, Sword-Saint of Japan, who was undefeated in more than sixty duels, many of which were to the death. He also authored the great philosophical work, *The Book of Five Rings*.

Now, one may say that this does not seem like an appropriate example of someone who would ever be considered ordinary, but let me make my point clear by quoting Eiji Yoshikawa, the Japanese historian and author of the epic novel *Musashi*, who explained this about his protagonist:

> I wouldn't say that Musashi is ordinary, but he is. That's what's extraordinary about him. He is not content to rely on whatever natural gifts he may have. Knowing he is ordinary; he is constantly trying to improve himself. No one appreciates the agonizing effort he's had to make. Now that his years of training have yielded such spectacular results, everybody's talking about his 'God-given talent.' That's how men who don't try very hard comfort themselves.

If the capacity for greatness is just a matter of genetic lottery, then it becomes an easy excuse for many to justify complacency. But Musashi's example demolishes this comfortable illusion. His greatness was not a gift, but an achievement—the result of countless hours of practice, study, and self-reflection. He understood something that many people refuse to accept: that within every ordinary person lies the potential for extraordinary development.

Musashi's approach was fundamentally philosophical. He didn't just train his body and his sword technique; he cultivated his mind and character. He studied strategy, not just as it applied to combat, but as it applied to life itself. He understood that true mastery requires integration—the harmonious development of physical skill, mental clarity, and spiritual discipline. This was a lesson stressed to him as a young man from a wise mentor offering brutally honest, but constructive criticism:

> That's what I meant when I said it's a pity about you. You were born with physical strength and fortitude, but you lack both knowledge and wisdom. While you managed to master a few of the more unfortunate features of the Way of the Samurai, you made no effort to acquire learning or virtue. People talk about combining the Way of Learning with the Way of the Samurai, but when properly combined, they aren't two—they're one.

Later in Musashi's life, after so many lessons learned and many great achievements, he never forgot that he was ordinary:

> Some, he felt, understood him. For their good wishes he was grateful; their admiration infused him with a sense of reverence. At the same time, he was being swept up on a wave of that frivolous sentiment called popularity. His reaction was almost one of fear, that the adulation might go to his head. He was, after all, only an ordinary man.

The Toughest Man Alive

Next, I want to talk about David Goggins. David Goggins is a Navy SEAL and has been called the toughest man alive. In addition to his accomplishments serving his country, he has had many more impressive personal achievements outside of the military that have required great mental and physical strength. Just a couple of examples are that he held the world record for most pull-ups in a 24-hour period (4,030) and he ran 203.5 miles in 48 hours, taking first place in a National Championship endurance race. He also has had many other impressive results in marathons, endurance tests, and authored the bestselling books *Can't Hurt Me* and *Never Finished*.

Many people who know of him now look at David Goggins and can't imagine that they could ever come close to achieving similar accomplishments that could be relevant to their own personal lives and goals. Many think that David Goggins and others like him are in large part born naturally gifted or talented.

However, this could not be further from reality. In fact, when David was in his twenties he was terribly out of shape, obese, weighing about three-hundred pounds. He was afraid of the water, couldn't swim—and then he decided he wanted to be, of all things, a Navy SEAL. The first time he tried to run, he barely made it a half mile before he quit. He initially failed to qualify for the Navy SEALs, but he kept trying, learning and improving before he eventually made it. He was not born exceptionally smart, strong, or talented; he simply kept learning and improving every day and refused to give up or stop progressing. He continues to challenge himself and improving himself today, both mentally and physically. He struggled in school and was practically illiterate into his late teen years, but today he has also become a best-selling author.

Goggins' transformation is one of the most dramatic examples possible of the principle that ordinary people can achieve extraordinary things. Here was a man who started from about as disadvantaged a position as possible; but through sheer force of will and commitment to self-transformation, he became one of the most physically and mentally tough individuals on the planet.

The most important aspect of Goggins' story is not in his physical achievements, as impressive as they are. The most important aspect is his mental transformation. He developed what he calls "callused mind"—the ability to push through discomfort, to embrace rather than avoid difficulty, to find strength in struggle itself. This mental toughness didn't come from some genetic gift or special talent. *It came from a philosophical decision:*

the decision to take complete responsibility for his own life and development, regardless of his starting point or circumstances. Goggins understood that he could either be a victim of his circumstances or the architect of his transformation.

WHO'S GONNA CARRY THE BOATS?

One rhetorical question that Goggins often yells out loud during his intense workouts is, "Who's gonna carry the boats?"

To be a Navy SEAL, one of the challenges that you have to be able to do is carry heavy boats over your head and shoulders with your team, which is extremely difficult. In addition, when water and sand inevitably get into the boats it makes the task even more difficult. To carry these boats and to be able to deal with the extra challenge of water and sand takes great mental and physical strength. If we don't have Navy SEALs with the extreme mental and physical strength that it takes to complete these types of challenges, we would have no one to carry the boats when needed or the ability needed to carry out their tasks and duties for which they are training.

Now, I understand that most of us are not Navy SEALs, but the boats are a metaphor for life. The sand and the water that will get in the boats are the extra metaphorical obstacles and difficulties that everyone inevitably faces throughout their lives. This metaphor cuts to the heart of what it means to live a philosophical life. Challenges will come—some predictable, some completely unexpected. The question is not whether you will face difficulties; the question is whether you will be prepared when they arrive. The boats represent all the responsibilities, challenges, and burdens that life inevitably places on our shoulders. They represent our principles and the duties we have to our families, our communities, and ourselves. They likewise represent the problems we must solve, the obstacles we must overcome, and the standards we must uphold. The sand and water represent the additional complications—the unexpected setbacks, the unfair circumstances—that make every challenge more difficult than it appears from the outside.

Struggling and suffering will always be part of life, so we should appropriately train and prepare ourselves both mentally and physically; and just as the physical aspect will involve exercise and training, the mental aspect must involve reading and studying.

Many people approach life assuming that someone else will carry the boats. They assume that the government will solve the big problems, that the police will provide security for them and their families. These are dangerous assumptions. The true philosopher understands that, ultimately, you are responsible for carrying your own boats to the best of your ability. You are responsible for developing your mental and physical strength. You are responsible for preparing yourself not just for the challenges you can foresee, but for the ones you can't even imagine yet.

So, like Goggins, I ask, who is going to carry the boats in your life? If you answer that you will yourself, then this book is for you.

The Ordinary Heroes Among Us

In my own life, I remember a time when I took a first aid course at a sportsman club. I walked in and took my seat and the instructor was in the front of the room dressed very modestly in a dirty old t-shirt and a worn-out pair of jeans. He certainly wasn't doing any special grooming to impress anyone with his hair or beard style. Despite his modest appearance and being relatively soft-spoken, he proceeded for the next two hours to teach a class of about twenty of us how to potentially save someone's life if they were suffering from a gunshot wound.

On my way home from this incredibly informative class where the instructor shared his knowledge and stories of previous military experience full of wisdom to consider, something struck me about the significance of his modest appearance. It reminded me of the lesson of "The Jolly Tailor." Outside of that classroom setting he was the kind of guy that we might see and walk past and hardly notice at all, let alone think of him as a heroic figure or a man of wisdom. But what this man was doing with his life was passing down vital knowledge and wisdom that could literally save lives. Without knowing anything more about that gentleman, he nevertheless had the knowledge and potential to act heroically and was passing that knowledge and some bit of wisdom along to others who would now potentially be able to save a life with their new knowledge.

This story illustrates perhaps the most important point of this entire introduction: heroism and wisdom are not always recognizable at first glance. Our culture has trained us to expect heroes to look like movie stars or professional athletes and wise men to look like professors in academic robes. We expect dramatic music and perfect lighting and inspiring speeches. But real heroism and real wisdom are more often found in quiet competence, in modest service, in the willingness to share what you know with those who need to know it.

The first-aid instructor was not seeking fame or recognition. He was not trying to impress anyone with his appearance or his credentials. He was simply doing what needed to be done: passing along knowledge that could save lives. This is what ordinary people who become extraordinary actually look like most of the time. They look ordinary. But they have taken the time and made the effort to develop extraordinary competence in areas that matter. They have prepared themselves to carry the boats when needed. *The heroic capability is not about external presentation but about internal preparation.* Wisdom is not about appearing wise but about wise action through knowledge, skill and virtue.

Our culture has been brainwashed and degraded to the point that we worship and idolize those with money, power, fame or status as heroic role models, for no other reason; in reality, it is quite often those who had the opportunity for money, power, fame or status and voluntarily sacrificed those things for a higher good who have been the real heroes.

For further investigation into these matters, see:

- Seneca, *On the Shortness of Life*
- Epictetus, *Discourses*
- Eiji Yoshikowa, *Musashi*
- Miyamoto Musashi, *The Book of Five Rings*
- David Goggins, *Can't Hurt Me*
- David Goggins, *Never Finished*

CHAPTER 2

PHILOSOPHY AS A WAY OF LIFE

In the same way that the true warrior trains daily and yearns for the day when his courage will be tested, even if it costs him his life, the true philosopher also trains daily and looks forward to the day when his virtues will be tested to see if he is deserving of the title, and if not, it will certainly be a certain kind of death.

It's worth considering that the subject of philosophy was once thought of as one of the four pillars of knowledge. In the early 1500's Raphael painted the four walls of the *Stanza della Segnatura* in the Apostolic Palace of the Vatican to represent four pillars of knowledge: philosophy, theology, poetry, and justice. At that time there was a lot that fell under the umbrella of philosophy (science, mathematics, etc.), but it's worth wondering why philosophy was once considered one of the four pillars of knowledge and yet the subject today has become relatively insignificant and ignored throughout our education system. To be honest, the general population of our current Western culture often scoffs at philosophy as a useless field of study.

This transformation didn't happen overnight. The gradual marginalization of philosophy represents one of the most tragic intellectual developments in Western civilization. When we examine Raphael's magnificent fresco "The School of Athens," or, as it is often referred to, "Philosophy," we see philosophy represented not as an abstract academic discipline, but as the very foundation of human inquiry. Aristotle and Plato stand at the center, surrounded by mathematicians, astronomers, and other thinkers—all united under the banner of philosophical investigation.

I previously looked at this painting as divided between Plato and Aristotle, but eventually I recognized the two sides as balanced and in *dialectic* with each other (the concept of dialectic is something we will go into greater detail about in Chapter 4). The brief point I want to make here is that in this painting you can sense the collaboration between great thinkers—the sharing of ideas and information in good faith, their sense of wonder, their thirst for knowledge and understanding—ultimately their search for *wisdom*. They are not yelling and arguing or debating with each other; rather, what we see is a good faith dialogue between various perspectives for each individual to become a little wiser. This painting represents the importance of philosophy and illustrates her true spirit.

The Practical Nature of Philosophy

Philosophy is about loving and seeking *wisdom* and learning how to think and communicate at the highest level *in alignment with virtue.*

When you think about the practicality of the subject of philosophy, is there any aspect of our lives, no matter who you are or what you do for a living, that you wouldn't want to maximize for yourself and those around you the ability to make wise decisions and to think and communicate well? If you're thinking something like, "Of course I would want to make wise decisions and think and communicate effectively," then you already intuitively understand why the subject of philosophy is both important and practical for everyone. Unfortunately, many have not realized that this is the proper role of philosophy and that it's a tragedy to neglect the search for wisdom and the practice of thinking and communicating at the highest level.

Much of this is due to a degenerate and failing education system where the subject of philosophy in K-12 is essentially nonexistent. Where it can be found in higher education today, much has become sophistry or just memorizing propositional knowledge for those who want to become philosophy professors. As Henry David Thoreau aptly states: "Nowadays, there are philosophy professors, but no philosophers."

The distinction is that professors teach history and facts about philosophers, while an actual philosopher is someone who lives out the philosophical life. I can teach a class about the history and ideas of Spartan warriors, but that obviously does not make me a Spartan warrior just because I studied and memorized some facts about them. There is no correlation between being a philosophy professor and living philosophically in the ancient sense.

The absence of proper philosophical education in our schools represents a massive failure of our education system. We teach young people mathematics, science, and history, but we don't teach them how to think clearly about the fundamental questions of human existence. We give them knowledge, but not wisdom; information, but not understanding; technique, but not judgment. The result is graduates who may be technically competent in their chosen field but who lack the intellectual framework necessary to navigate life's deeper challenges wisely. They can solve mathematical equations, but struggle to solve moral dilemmas. They may be able to analyze literary texts, but can't analyze their own beliefs and assumptions. They can memorize historical facts, but struggle to learn from history's lessons about human nature and social organization. As Daniel Schmachtenberger says in one of the great, albeit lesser-known quotes of our current times, "STEM makes people who are great weapons, but doesn't make people who can see where the system is being weaponized."

Furthermore, and adding to the focus on developing philosophy professors rather than cultivating a culture of actual philosophers, is what philosophy is not: philosophy is not a course of study to take on for the sole purpose of financial gain. As Friedrich Nietzsche proclaimed, "If we reduce the value of higher education to the material return on our financial investment, we will impoverish our culture and diminish ourselves."

Similarly, in the *Apology* Socrates compares the sale of wisdom to the sale of sexual favors. It seems to me to be true that the greatest things in life are free (Plato would say Goodness, Truth, and Beauty) and this is why it is only fitting that studying the great subject of philosophy is not motivated by material/financial profits and that higher virtues are worth contemplating and pursuing.

This point cannot be overemphasized in our materialistic age. When wisdom becomes a commodity to be bought and sold, it ceases to be wisdom and becomes something else entirely—perhaps information, perhaps technique, perhaps entertainment, but not wisdom. Wisdom is not a product that can be packaged and delivered; it is a *way of being* that must be cultivated through sustained practice and commitment.

The moment someone begins studying philosophy primarily for career advancement or financial gain, they have already missed the point. They may acquire philosophical knowledge, they may learn to speak the language of philosophy, they may even become professionally successful philosophy professors or consultants, but they will likely not become wise.

This is not to say that philosophical training cannot provide practical benefits or that philosophers should live in poverty. The point is that these secondary benefits cannot be the primary motivation without corrupting the entire enterprise. When you love wisdom for its own sake, you often find that it provides practical benefits as well—better decision-making, clearer thinking, meaning in life, inner peace, and greater resilience in the face of difficulty. These are the kinds of gifts that philosophy has to offer and the kinds of gifts that our education system is failing to offer our children.

Philosopher and educator Mortimer J. Adler observed this phenomenon in the early 1950s:

> Our education has undergone so drastic a process of dilution that we are ill-equipped, even after graduation from a respectable college, to tackle anything much above the level of the comic book.

> The decay of education in the West, which is felt most profoundly in America, undoubtedly makes the task of understanding these books more difficult than it was for earlier generations. In fact, my observation leads me to the horrid suspicion that these books are easier for people who have had no formal education than they are for those who have acquired that combination of misinformation, unphilosophy, and slipshod habits that is the usual result of the most elaborate and expensive institutional education in America.

As a result, many people today have a perception of philosophy that is something like "intellectuals" in a room at some ivy league school somewhere sitting around and theorizing about abstract thoughts that don't seem to have much practicality in our everyday lives. While there is nothing wrong with sitting in a room and theorizing abstract thoughts—and this is certainly one aspect of philosophy—there is so much more.

Philosophy is not a hobby, but a responsibility.

Consider the daily challenges that every person faces: How should I spend my limited time? What career should I pursue? How should I raise my children? What do I owe to my community? How should I respond to suffering—my own and others'? What gives life meaning? These are not just abstract theoretical questions—they are the most practical questions imaginable. They are all, at their core, philosophical questions. Every answer you give to these questions reflects philosophical assumptions about human nature, the good life, justice, truth, and meaning. Most people operate with philosophical frameworks they've never consciously chosen or carefully examined. They've absorbed these frameworks from their culture, their family, their peer groups, or their media consumption. The tragedy is that unexamined philosophical assumptions often lead to inconsistent, self-deceptive, and harmful patterns of living.

Sophistry: The Counterfeit of Philosophy

Another reason for the negative public impression that has developed in regards to this subject comes from the fact that most things of value will inevitably have a counterfeit. This is obvious with more materialistic examples such as counterfeit golf clubs, money, etc. This is a way for swindlers and "snake oil salesmen" to make a dishonest profit from the unwitting. Philosophy is no different, but its counterfeits cannot only be used for financial profit, but even more so to manipulate the masses and lead the unwitting down a dangerous path that can lead to tyranny, intellectual bankruptcy, nihilism. and any number of catastrophic scenarios.

Throughout the history of philosophy, these types are referred to as sophists. Sophistry has been described as "that which looks like philosophy, but is not." Sophists often excel at creating elaborate theoretical constructions that sound profound, but often lack nuance, are misleading or just outright lies. They use technical jargon to intimidate rather than illuminate. They engage in intellectual showmanship rather than honest inquiry. Most dangerously, they often attract followers who mistake complexity for depth and verbal cleverness for wisdom. It is important to understand that sophistry is the counterfeit of philosophy. It is important that we take responsibility and develop the *wisdom* needed to identify the distinction between sophistry and philosophy.

Plato was well aware of the dangers of philosophy falling into the wrong hands. This is why he and other ancient philosophers insisted that character development *must* precede intellectual development in an attempt to prevent this misuse of philosophy.

> There is danger lest they should taste the dear delight too early; for youngsters, as you may have observed, when they first get the taste in

> their mouths, argue for amusement, and are always contradicting and refuting others in imitation of those who refute them; like puppy-dogs, they rejoice in pulling and tearing at all who come near them. (*The Republic* VII [539])

A person of poor character will use whatever intellectual tools they can acquire in service of their existing prejudices and appetites. They can become more sophisticated in their self-deception, more skillful in their manipulation of others, more dangerous in their ignorance. The sophistication becomes a weapon for manipulation rather than a tool for achieving truth and wisdom. Philosophical ideas, when stripped of their ethical foundations and divorced from the pursuit of wisdom, can become instruments of evil.

Plato's hope was that with proper character development starting at young age that students would grow into young men who would use their philosophical training virtuously:

> But when a man begins to get older, he will no longer be guilty of such insanity; he will imitate the dialectician who is seeking for truth, and not the eristic, who is contradicting for the sake of amusement; and the greater moderation of his character will increase instead of diminishing the honour of the pursuit. (*The Republic* VII [539])

Unfortunately, we have to a large degree skipped this early philosophical training of prioritizing character development, and our culture and politics have become corrupted with sophistry and grown adults by age only, involved in politics and academics that act like "puppy-dogs" as they rejoice in their pulling and tearing at all who come near them.

Too many people today have been exposed to sophistry rather than philosophy and they intuitively have a repulsion for the fancy talking, mental gymnastics, nonsense and outright lies which don't seem to follow logically, rationally or be practically useful or relevant in their everyday lives; and therefore many people have developed a bad impression of what they think philosophy is.

The reality is, Plato can and has been twisted into fascism, and Aristotle can and has been twisted into "Scientism"; the concepts of Natural Law and biblical texts can and have been twisted into tyranny. Those who do so may often be labeled as intellectuals/philosophers, but they can never be called wise. The ethos of any society that does not prioritize wisdom at its foundation is doomed to fail. Wisdom is that which allows one to recognize the Good, the True and the Beautiful, without falling for their imposters.

Again, this is why we all must take the responsibility on ourselves for philosophical training and cultivating the wisdom to recognize the difference between true philosophy and sophistry; to "carry our boats," we might say.

Philo-Sophia: To Seek and to Love Wisdom

There is only one philosophy—that which is dedicated to seeking, loving and understanding wisdom with a teleology of self-transformation, a lived wisdom and inner peace in accordance with the logos above all else. Anything else is sophism (fallacious/ deceiving).

The Greek roots of the word "philosophy" tell us everything we need to know about its proper nature. "Philo" means love—not casual affection, but a deep, passionate, committed love. "Sophia" means wisdom—not mere cleverness or information, but the integrated understanding that enables right living. Philosophy is literally the love of wisdom; and, like all genuine love, it transforms both the lover and the beloved.

This love of wisdom is not a passive sentiment, but an active orientation toward life. It is a *way of being* in the world that prioritizes truth over comfort, understanding over certainty, and growth over stagnation. The philosophical person is one who has made a fundamental commitment to follow the argument wherever it leads, to change their mind when presented with better evidence, and to seek and to love wisdom.

The teleology—the ultimate goal—of philosophy is self-transformation towards the Good, the True, and the Beautiful. This is what distinguishes genuine philosophy from mere intellectual exercise. The point is not to accumulate philosophical knowledge, but to become a philosophical person. The point is not to win arguments, but to become wiser. The point is not to impress others with your intellectual sophistication, but to live a life worthy of a rational, ethical being.

Therefore, to call oneself a philosopher is first and foremost the recognition and the admission of one's own ignorance and insufficiencies. It is this recognition that is the impetus to a *way of life* that is dedicated to seeking wisdom, specifically through the dialectic process, with the telos of living a virtuous life, self-transformation, and arriving at an inner peace in alignment with the logos above all else.

This is perhaps the most counterintuitive aspect of philosophy for modern readers. In our culture, we expect experts to claim knowledge, authorities to demonstrate certainty, teachers to provide answers. But the philosophical approach begins with the Socratic recognition of just how much we do not know. This is not false modesty or intellectual cowardice—it is the beginning of all genuine learning.

When you truly understand how much you don't know, you can become hungry for knowledge. When you recognize your own limitations, you become open to growth. When you acknowledge your own mistakes, you become capable of correction. The person who thinks they already know everything has closed themselves off from further learning. Only the person who recognizes their ignorance can move closer towards wisdom. But this admission of ignorance is not an end in itself—it is the beginning of a lifelong journey. Philosophy is not a static state but a dynamic process; not a destination but a way of traveling. It requires the courage to question your deepest beliefs, the humility to change your mind when necessary and the ego to know you can become better.

Does Philosophy Offer Answers to Life's Questions?

Another thing that frustrates many people about philosophy is actually a hint about its hidden treasures. Philosophy often doesn't seem to actually answer any of life's most significant questions in any specific or definitive way; often, any answers that are proposed may initially seem unfulfilling, insufficient, or ambiguous.

This frustration stems from a misunderstanding of the proper role of philosophy. In simple terms, philosophy is about *how to think* for oneself, not *what* to think. As the famous sentiment of Socrates goes, "I cannot teach anybody anything, I can only make them think."

This frustration is perfectly understandable. We live in a culture that values quick fixes, simple solutions, and step-by-step instructions. We want to know exactly what to do in every situation, exactly what to believe about every issue, exactly how to solve every problem. When philosophy refuses to provide these simple answers, it can seem useless or even deliberately obscure.

But this apparent weakness of philosophy is actually its greatest strength. Human existence is irreducibly complex, filled with genuine dilemmas that admit of no easy solutions. The questions that matter most—How should I live? What do I owe to others? What gives life meaning?—cannot be answered by consulting a manual or following a formula.

Philosophy teaches us something more valuable than specific answers: it teaches us how to think about these questions in increasingly sophisticated ways. It develops our capacity for judgment, our ability to see situations clearly, our skill at weighing competing considerations and making wise decisions even in novel circumstances. As Victor Frankl writes in *Man's Search for Meaning*:

> To put the question in general terms would be comparable to the question posed to a chess champion: 'Tell me, Master, what is the best move in the world?' There simply is no such thing as the best or even a good move apart from a particular situation in a game and the particular personality of one's opponent. The same holds for human existence.

This analogy perfectly captures the nature of philosophical wisdom. A chess master doesn't succeed because he has memorized the "correct" response to every possible situation—there are too many possible combinations for that to be feasible. Instead, he has developed the ability to see patterns, to understand principles, to think strategically, and to adapt to novel situations. He has trained his judgment.

Philosophy works the same way. It doesn't give you a rulebook for life because life is too complex and variable for any rulebook to be adequate. Instead, it trains your philosophical judgment. It develops your ability to see clearly, think deeply, and choose wisely in whatever circumstances you find yourself. This is why philosophical education remains relevant across centuries and cultures—the specific situations change, but the need for good judgment remains constant.

The philosopher learns to ask better questions, rather than providing final answers. What are the assumptions underlying this belief? What are the implications of this action? What are the competing values at stake in this decision? How might this look from a different perspective? These questions don't solve problems mechanically, but they illuminate problems in ways that make wise solutions more likely.

I can use Socrates and Aristotle as perfect examples. Although Socrates refused to apologize for his allegations (impiety and corrupting the youth), he decided not to flee when the opportunity presented itself – an opportunity that could have potentially saved his life. He drank the poison hemlock after he was found guilty at his trial:

> When he was defending himself against the charge brought by Meletus, although other people in the lawcourts normally gratify the jurors by the way they talk and flatter and beg, in violation of the laws, and although through such means many have often been acquitted by the jurors, he refused to do in violation of the laws any of the things normal in the lawcourt; on the contrary, although he would easily have

been acquitted by the jurors if he had made even a modest attempt at any of those things, he preferred death through obeying the laws to life through breaking them. (*The Apology*)

He would say, "I need to escape this charge by the means that is most clearly just, by informing you of the truth, not by trickery." Mortimer Adler has pointed out that Aristotle, when faced with similar circumstances:

> Charged with impiety for the elegy he had written to Hermias twenty years before, Aristotle recalled the fate of Socrates and fled to his mother's property in Chalcis, declaring, 'I will not let the Athenians offend twice against philosophy.'

Although both men made very different decisions under *similar* circumstances, the case could be made that they both made the "right" or even the wise decision, based on the particulars of their individual lives and circumstances.

These two examples perfectly illustrate why philosophy cannot provide universal formulae for living. Both Socrates and Aristotle were profound philosophical thinkers who understood virtue, justice, and the good life. Yet when faced with similar external circumstances, they made completely different choices—and both choices can be defended as wise.

Socrates chose to stay and face death because, for him, in his circumstances, with his mission and his character, this was the most authentic expression of his philosophical life. He had spent his entire career questioning others about virtue and justice—how could he abandon those principles when his own life was on the line? His death became the ultimate philosophical argument, a demonstration that some things are more important than mere biological survival.

Aristotle chose to flee because, for him in his circumstances, with his different mission and character, preservation of his life meant the preservation of his philosophical work. He could better serve philosophy and the pursuit of wisdom by living to continue his teaching and writing than by dying for a principle. His extensive body of work, which has influenced Western thought for over two millennia, is a good justification for his decision.

This is the paradox of philosophical wisdom: it is both universal and particular, both eternal and temporal. The principles of wisdom are universal—honesty, courage, justice, temperance—but their application must always be sensitive to particular circumstances, individual character, and unique situations.

This can cause a sense of *aporia* that is a key characteristic of Socratic dialectic that is often experienced at the end of Plato's dialogues—meaning, you may have a sense of inner conflict, you may recognize the natural ambiguity that is present in many of life's questions and answers, yet still somehow a deeper sense and understanding of the *essence* of the issues seems to present itself through the dialectic process. Again, in the spirit of "I cannot teach anyone anything, I can only make them think." This is the essence of the dialectic process which we will discuss in more detail later in the text.

Aporia—this state of puzzlement, perplexity or potential inner conflict—is not a failure of philosophy. When you finish reading a Platonic dialogue and feel more confused than when you started, this confusion is not a sign that you haven't understood the dialogue. In fact, it may be a sign that you have understood it perfectly. You are experiencing what Socrates intended you to experience: the recognition that the issue at hand is more complex and more profound than you may have initially realized.

This can be deeply unsettling for those who are used to getting clear, definitive answers. But this unsettling quality is precisely what makes philosophy so valuable. Aporia forces you to think more deeply, to question your assumptions, to remain humble in the face of complexity. It prevents you from settling for easy answers to difficult questions. It keeps you intellectually honest.

The person who has never experienced aporia is the person who has never truly engaged with philosophy. They may have memorized philosophical facts, they may be able to recite philosophical arguments, but they have not been transformed by philosophical thinking. They are still operating under the assumption that every question has a simple answer, that every problem has a straightforward solution. As cognitive scientist and philosopher John Vervaeke explains, "You do not teach anyone philosophy; you present to them a beautiful way of life."

If you have not yet picked up on the *essence* of philosophy you may ask, "Okay great, what exactly is this beautiful way of life?" If you have begun to understand the essence of philosophy you will understand that the idea is that if you do your due diligence and dedicate yourself to a virtuous life, seeking and loving wisdom, a beautiful way of life will reveal itself to you.

Philosophy cannot be reduced to a set of rules or prescriptions because it is not a system to be learned, but a way of being to be embodied. It is not a destination to arrive at, but a path to walk. The beautiful way of life that philosophy offers cannot be described in advance because it is different for each person who walks the philosophical path.

What can be said is that this way of life is characterized by certain qualities: intellectual humility combined with moral courage; openness to truth combined with commitment to what you discover to be true; and the pursuit of wisdom. It is a life lived in accordance with reason while remaining sensitive to the limits of reason.

The beauty of this way of life is not the beauty of ease or comfort—indeed, it often requires significant sacrifice and can be quite demanding. It is beautiful because it is authentic, because it leads to genuine human flourishing, and because it develops what is highest and best in human nature. It is the beauty of a life lived in pursuit of Truth, Goodness, and Beauty themselves.

Wisdom and Philosophy as a Woman

Throughout history, wisdom and philosophy have been symbolized as a woman. In his *Thus Spoke Zarathustra*, Nietzsche writes, "Careless, mocking, forceful—so does wisdom wish us: she is a woman, and never loves anyone but a warrior." In *The Consolation of Philosophy*, Philosophy comes to visit Boethius in the form of a woman:

> While I was thinking these thoughts to myself in silence, and set my pen to record this tearful complaint, there seemed to stand above my head a woman. Her look filled me with awe; her burning eyes penetrated more deeply than those of ordinary men; her complexion was fresh with an ever-lively bloom, yet she seemed so ancient that none would think her of our time.

This feminine symbolism for philosophy and wisdom appears across cultures and throughout history. From the Hebrew Bible's personification of wisdom as a woman who calls out in the streets, to the Greek goddess Athena who represents both wisdom and war, to the medieval allegories where Philosophy appears as a woman of great beauty and terrible power—this imagery points to something profound about the nature of wisdom itself.

The feminine symbolism suggests that wisdom must be courted rather than conquered, won through devotion rather than domination. Wisdom cannot be forced or manipulated into revealing herself. She responds only to genuine love, to sincere seeking, to authentic dedication. Like any profound relationship, the relationship with wisdom requires patience, faithfulness, and commitment. Otherwise, you end up with a relationship that is something more like prostitution—sophistry.

The characterization of wisdom as "careless, mocking, forceful" may seem surprising, but it accurately captures something essential about the philosophical experience. Wisdom is careless about our ego concerns, our desires for status or comfort or easy answers. Wisdom mocks our pretensions, our assumption that we already know what we need to know. Wisdom can be forceful in demanding that we abandon our illusions and face reality as it actually is, not as we wish it were.

Again, the word "philosophy," derived from the Greek words Philo and Sophia, translates to loving or seeking wisdom. If we advance the metaphor of wisdom as a woman:

What is more natural, more right, more necessary than for man to seek and love a woman so that we can reproduce the wisdom needed to pass along to the future generations? But if men, if those with the warrior spirit stop seeking, stop loving, stop participating with philosophy and stop loving and seeking wisdom, our culture will lose invaluable wisdom; we will be unable to reproduce the much-needed wisdom for future generations.

This metaphor operates on multiple levels simultaneously. On the most literal level, it suggests that *the pursuit of wisdom is as natural and necessary as the human drive toward love and procreation. Just as a culture that ceases to reproduce biologically will die out, a culture that ceases to reproduce wisdom will perish intellectually and morally.*

But the metaphor goes deeper than a biological analogy. The relationship between the seeker and wisdom mirrors the relationship between lover and beloved in its intensity, its demands, and its transformative power. Those who truly love wisdom find that wisdom changes them fundamentally. They cannot remain the same person they were before wisdom entered their lives.

The reference to "those with the warrior spirit" is crucial here. Wisdom "never loves anyone but a warrior" because only the warrior spirit has the courage to face difficult truths, to endure the struggle of genuine learning, to persist when the path becomes difficult. The warrior mentality is not just about aggression or violence, but about discipline, courage, and the willingness to engage in difficult battles appropriately—including and especially the battle with oneself.

In our current cultural moment, when both genuine scholarship and authentic courage are in short supply, this metaphor takes on special urgency. We are witnessing what happens when cultures abandon the pursuit of wisdom—intellectual confusion, moral decay, social fragmentation, and the rise of sophistical manipulation masquerading as leadership.

The Scholar-Warrior Ideal

Furthermore, an important quote attributed to the ancient historian, Thucydides, argues that: *"The nation that makes a great distinction between its scholars and its warriors will have its thinking done by cowards and its fighting done by fools."*

Unfortunately, at our current point in time, our culture has not done a very good job of cultivating either scholars or warriors, let alone the ideal synthesis alluded to by Thucydides.

This observation points to one of the most serious problems in contemporary culture: the artificial separation of the scholar from moral virtue and physical strength. On one side, we have intellectuals who can analyze and theorize but lack the courage or practical wisdom to apply their insights to real-world problems. They retreat into academic jargon and abstract speculation, becoming increasingly disconnected from the concerns of ordinary people. Their thinking, however sophisticated, remains sterile because it is not grounded in moral commitment.

On the other side, we have people of action who operate from instinct and emotion but lack the intellectual tools to think clearly about complex problems. They may have courage, good intentions and strong convictions, but without the discipline of rigorous thinking, they often end up causing more harm than good. Their actions, however well-intentioned, remain crude because they are not guided by wisdom and understanding.

What the great philosophical traditions have always advocated is the integration of these two aspects of human excellence. We need thinking that is grounded in moral commitment and action that is guided by intellectual clarity and wisdom. We need scholar-warriors: people who can think deeply and act courageously, who combine intellectual rigor with moral integrity and physical strength and courage.

It's important to observe that this concept of the synthesis of the scholar/philosopher and the warrior has been a common thread among ancient philosophers. Socrates was known to be a courageous soldier. "Plato" was actually a wrestling nickname that meant broad shoulders (his real name was Aristocles). Alexander the Great famously studied under Aristotle. Think of Marcus Aurelius as the Emperor of Rome. As previously mentioned, Miyamoto Musashi who fought over sixty duels, many of which were to the death, but he was also a great philosophical mind. And let's not forget: he was an ordinary man.

These examples are not coincidental. They reflect a deep understanding that intellectual, physical, and moral courage are not separate virtues but different aspects of the same underlying excellence. The person who can face difficult truths in the realm of ideas is the same person who can face difficult challenges in the realm of action. The discipline required for rigorous thinking is the same discipline required for ethical living. The courage needed to question popular beliefs is the same courage needed to stand up for what is right.

Consider Marcus Aurelius. Here was a man who held the most powerful position in the world—Emperor of Rome—yet who spent his private moments writing philosophical reflections that reveal a profound commitment to virtue and wisdom. His *Meditations* show us what it looks like when philosophical training meets practical responsibility, when the love of wisdom guides the exercise of power.

In the same way that the true warrior trains daily and yearns for the day when his courage will be tested, even if it costs him his life, the true philosopher also trains daily and looks forward to the day when his virtues will be tested to see if he is deserving of the title, and if not, it will certainly be a certain kind of death. Who could be more honorable, more noble, than a wise and virtuous warrior? This is where the cultivation of a strong, healthy, resilient culture must begin. This is what we as individuals and collectively can begin to aim for today.

Every day presents opportunities to choose wisdom over comfort, truth over convenience, virtue over expedience. Every conversation is a chance to practice dialectical engagement. Every decision is an opportunity to apply philosophical principles to practical circumstances. Every challenge is a test of whether one's philosophical education has produced genuine wisdom or mere cleverness.

The "death" that awaits the philosopher who fails these tests is not physical but spiritual—the death of intellectual integrity, the death of moral courage, the death of the very qualities that make philosophical life worth living. This is why character development must precede and accompany intellectual development in any serious philosophical education. Without virtue, philosophy becomes sophistry; without seeking wisdom, learning becomes mere information gathering without a proper aim.

This is indeed where the cultivation of a strong, healthy, resilient culture must begin—with individuals who have committed themselves to the lifelong pursuit of wisdom and virtue, who have trained themselves to think clearly and act courageously, who understand that the greatest battles are often fought not only on physical battlefields but in the realm of ideas, the development of character, in our everyday life decisions. The paradigm shift we desperately need begins with ordinary men who voluntarily choose to *carry the boats*.

For further investigation into philosophy:

- John Vervaeke, (YouTube series) *Awakening from the Meaning Crisis*

- Pierre Hadot, *What Is Ancient Philosophy?*

- Pierre Hadot, *Philosophy as a Way of Life*

- Plato, *Apology*

- Plato, *Phaedo*

- Marcus Aurelius, *Meditations*

- Darrell Huff, *How to Lie with Statistics*

CHAPTER 3

WISDOM OVER INTELLIGENCE

Wisdom is that which allows one to recognize the Good, the True and the Beautiful without falling for their imposters.

What is wisdom?

Wisdom is... well, one of those concepts that exposes the limitations of language, that defies a perfectly precise reductive definition. However, I propose we all carry at least some intuitive understanding of wisdom. Throughout history the archetype of "The Wise Old Man" has appeared in our stories, myths, and films. When we watch a movie, we intuitively recognize exactly who this wise figure is even if we may not be able to find the perfect language to describe them in a way that would fully encompass the concept of wisdom. This figure is not synonymous with someone who has memorized vast amounts of information. He is not typically some rich celebrity, entertainer or sports person. He is something else entirely—someone who has learned not just how to know, but how to be. This figure is often very "ordinary" looking, such as the *jolly tailer* that we discussed in the introduction. For just a couple of examples:

Socrates—Perhaps the most perfect historical example of this archetype. Socrates was not a wealthy man, held no official position, owned no school, and wrote nothing down. To the casual observer in ancient Athens, he appeared as an odd, barefoot philosopher wandering the marketplace, engaging whomever would talk with him. His appearance was famously unprepossessing—described as ugly, with a snub nose and protruding eyes. Yet this seemingly ordinary man possessed such wisdom that the Oracle of Delphi declared no one wiser. He valued truth over comfort and ultimately chose death rather than compromise his principles. Socrates never sought power or status; he sought only to help others—and himself—to move closer to wisdom.

Mr. Miyagi from *The Karate Kid*—Though fictional, this character perfectly illustrates the archetype for modern audiences. At first glance, Miyagi appears to be nothing more than a humble apartment handyman—an elderly immigrant doing menial maintenance work. Daniel initially fails to see anything special about him. Yet this unassuming figure possesses profound martial arts mastery and, more importantly, deep wisdom about life itself. His teaching methods seem strange, even absurd: wax on, wax off, paint the fence, sand the floor. Only later does the deeper meaning reveal itself.

Miyagi never boasts of his abilities, holds no official rank or position, owns no dojo, and lives simply. He has faced suffering and loss, yet maintains equanimity. He embodies what he teaches.

Oddly enough, even though we seem to have this intuition, or you could say *memory* inside of us, to recognize these figures from a "zoomed out" perspective (movies, books, etc.), so often we seem to forget this during our own everyday lives and interactions. (This idea of an intuition/memory of wisdom is an important note. In the next chapter on dialectic, I will highlight that one characteristic of the dialectic process, is that it can help us *remember).*

We have become part of a culture that obsesses over the shallow and superficial, such as celebrities, sports stars, actors/entertainers, etc. for no reason other than their popularity and wealth, while we seem to have forgotten all about the concept of wisdom. It has been a relatively modern phenomenon that cultures have basically began to worship and look up to athletes, celebrities and entertainers as role models.

In Ancient Rome for example, actors (*histriones*) were considered *infames*—a legal category that included prostitutes, gladiators, and pimps. In ancient Rome, *infames* were people who had lost their legal or social standing due to certain types of behavior, profession, or punishment.

The word literally means "ill-famed" or "disgraced." To be declared *infamis* meant that a person's reputation and civic rights were officially damaged — they were no longer considered fully "honorable" members of Roman society. They couldn't vote, hold public office, or even be buried in certain areas. This was despite theater's popularity and some actors achieving wealth and fame. Today we largely see the inversion of this.

I'm certainly not suggesting that we adopt these same laws today or that there is anything wrong with being an actor, entertainer, or sports star, but I am suggesting that we need a paradigm shift in who and why we are propping certain people up in our culture as influential role models and people to admire, based solely on status or popularity. I'm suggesting we need to shift away from things like popularity, status, and wealth and focus more on things like honorability, courage and wisdom—focus more on the virtues of an individual.

Are we losing some of this inherent wisdom? Where are these wise old men in our culture today? Would we even recognize them if we met them in person?

In a culture that worships intelligence over wisdom, credentials over character, information over insight, we may have lost the ability to recognize wisdom when we encounter it. We celebrate those who speak cleverly rather than those who speak wisely. We elevate those with impressive professional resumes rather than those with developed character. We follow those who promise easy answers rather than those who ask difficult questions.

As John Vervaeke has put it simply, *"We are in the midst of a wisdom famine."* This may seem like a harsh assessment, but consider: How many highly intelligent people seem to be making foolish decisions? How many educated experts have led us astray?

The Intelligence Trap

I want to make sure I give appropriate recognition to cognitive scientist and philosopher John Vervaeke who has done some great in-depth work on this specifically, and I am paraphrasing from some of his work here. I will also reference his book as well as some others at the end of this chapter for further investigation into the topic.

Intelligence is the antidote to ignorance; Wisdom is the antidote to foolishness.

The recognition of the distinction between intelligence and wisdom is ancient. Plato warned against mistaking cleverness for wisdom, and the difference between knowledge and wisdom appears throughout philosophical tradition.

I'm actually not very impressed when I hear "so and so is so smart" or "so and so is so intelligent." Sure, these are valuable capacities, but they tell us nothing about whether a person is good, honest, courageous, or wise. They don't tell us if someone is a good parent, a good spouse, a trustworthy friend, or a just leader. Contrary to popular belief, being intelligent is also not a good indicator for whether or not someone is actually correct about any given topic.

As Vervaeke explains: *"There is no contradiction between being highly intelligent and being profoundly foolish. The very processes that make us intelligent problem solvers—that make us so adaptive—are the same processes that make us prone to self-deceptive and self-destructive behavior. You don't get one without the other."*

Highly intelligent people are often the most difficult to get to change their minds; it can be even more difficult for them to notice their own flawed thinking, specifically because they have the "mental gymnastics" skills (the intelligence) to justify themselves and convince themselves of just about anything when they put their minds to it. Without the philosophical tools to correct themselves, a highly intelligent person can build a case like a skilled lawyer and convince themselves and others of completely irrational nonsense.

This is one of the most dangerous misunderstandings of our age: the assumption that intelligence alone is sufficient for navigating life's complexities. We have been taught the importance of IQ scores, academic credentials, and technical expertise while neglecting the cultivation of wisdom. The ratio of conversations that take place about IQ/intelligence vs. wisdom is profoundly lopsided in the favor of intelligence. This is an example of where we need paradigm shift thinking. When the wisdom piece is neglected, the result is a civilization run by highly intelligent fools.

More dangerously, intelligence can be weaponized in service of foolishness. Again, to reemphasize Daniel Schmachtenberger's point from the previous chapter: "STEM makes people who are great weapons, but doesn't make people who can see where the system is being weaponized."

Consider what intelligence actually gives us: the ability to process information, to recognize patterns, to solve technical problems, to easily manipulate symbols and concepts. The intelligent person who lacks wisdom becomes sophisticated in their self-deception, more skillful in rationalizing their errors, more capable of constructing elaborate justifications for harmful actions. They can build impressive-sounding arguments for terrible ideas. They can use their cognitive abilities to manipulate others and themselves.

In addition, and something that I haven't heard anyone discuss, is what I propose is another major insufficiency of IQ type tests—that the questions typically have no emotional relevance. Why is this such an issue? Because human beings are first and foremost ruled by our emotions/intuitions and the number of significant real-world issues needing to be solved that are emotionally neutral is exactly ZERO. This is one reason why you can often observe people who seem very intelligent in some very narrow area of expertise—scientists, mathematicians, other academics, etc.—but once they become involved in controversial political or social topics, they seem to immediately abandon all epistemological integrity and become tribal, emotional and irrational. As Carl Jung has pointed out, "The discrepancy between intellect and feeling, which get in each other's way at the best of times, is a particularly painful chapter in the history of the human psyche."

If IQ tests included problem solving that strategically appealed to people's emotions (like actual problem solving in the real-world does) instead of emotionally neutral questioning, the dangerous insufficiency of current IQ testing for real world problem solving would quickly become apparent and many who can currently brag about their high academic test scores and credentials would instead fail miserably. To be clear, I am not saying that IQ testing is useless or that we should ignore intelligence, but I am saying that the paradigm shift in thinking must be first and foremost cultivation and prioritization for wisdom.

The intelligent fool is more dangerous than the simple fool because they have greater capacity for harm. History provides countless examples: brilliant ideologues who constructed sophisticated philosophical systems that justify tyranny; technical experts whose narrow focus led to catastrophic unintended consequences; educated elites who insulated themselves from recognizing their own biases; clever manipulators who used their cognitive abilities to exploit others.

Intelligence can answer "Can we do this?" Wisdom asks "Should we do this?" Wisdom seeks righteousness.

Different Ways of Knowing

Wisdom is not just knowledge. It is not just intelligence. It is not just information or data or facts. Wisdom is something that must be expressed through all types of knowing—through what cognitive science identifies as distinct forms: *propositional knowing* (knowing facts and truths), *procedural knowing* (knowing how to do something), *perspectival knowing* (the stance from which you understand), and *participatory knowing* (knowing through relationship and transformation). Wisdom requires the integration of all these types, which is why it cannot be reduced to mere intelligence or information.

Some characteristics of wisdom

This is not an exhaustive list, but wisdom does seem to have several essential characteristics:

First, and perhaps most fundamentally, *wisdom begins not only in wonder, as Socrates proclaimed, but in the development of virtue.* This is why Plato insisted that character development must precede intellectual development. You cannot become wise through study alone if your character remains undeveloped. A foolish person may be clever, may be knowledgeable, may even be intelligent—but they cannot be wise. Wisdom and virtue are inseparable.

Second, *wisdom implies action.* You cannot be wise in theory alone. There is a fundamental distinction between propositional knowing (knowing *that* something is true) and procedural knowing (knowing *how* to do something). A philosophy professor may know all the propositional truths about virtue—may be able to recite every philosophical argument about courage, justice, and temperance—yet live in a way that embodies none of these virtues. Wisdom is not having knowledge about virtue; it is *acting* virtuously.

Consider the difference between memorizing surfing techniques vs. actually surfing a wave. No amount of propositional knowledge—no matter how technically accurate—will enable you to balance through a tube. Wisdom works the same way. You don't gain wisdom from information alone, any more than you gain surfing ability from reading about surfing. We live at a time when we are all drowning in information, while being dangerously insufficient in wisdom.

Third, *wisdom cannot be misused*. We recognize that knowledge and skill can be put to evil purposes. Scientific knowledge can create weapons. Technical skill can be used for manipulation. But we do not think a person wise unless they act wisely. To act wisely is to act well. This is why those who twist philosophy into tyranny, however intellectually sophisticated they may be, can never be called wise.

Finally, *wisdom involves the ability to zero in on what is relevant*. This is enhanced relevance realization—the capacity to see what matters in a situation where countless factors compete for attention. The intelligent person can process the information. The wise person knows which information matters. As Vervaeke argues:

> You know what wisdom is ultimately? In very complex situations it's the ability to zero in on the relevant information, often requiring insight, and shape yourself (your agency) so that you're best fitted to that, so that you can intervene in that situation better than any other person could. That's wisdom. That's enhanced relevance

realization. That's what Neoplatonism promises you with an enhanced sense of connectedness.

These are not all-encompassing, scientific reductionist explanations or definitions, but this should be a foundation to at least begin to recognize the importance of this concept we call wisdom and hopefully incite a sense of wonder for further investigation.

The Crisis of Modern Education

Our current educational crisis is not merely a failure to teach wisdom—it is the systematic cultivation of its opposite. We have created a system that produces what Nietzsche warned against: highly trained specialists who lack any sense of the whole, any understanding of what makes life worth living. As Friedrich Nietzsche proclaimed, "If we reduce the value of higher education to the material return on our financial investment, we will impoverish our culture and diminish ourselves."

Education has largely been reduced to specialized job training, rather than creating well-rounded and virtuous human beings. Knowledge has been commodified. Intelligence has been weaponized for marketplace competition. We have reduced everything to education for the sake of economic means.

The absence of proper philosophical education in our schools represents a massive failure. We teach young people facts about mathematics, science, history, etc., but we don't teach them how to think clearly about the fundamental questions of human existence. We give them knowledge but not wisdom, information but not understanding, technique but not judgment. The result is graduates who may be technically competent in their chosen fields but who lack the intellectual framework necessary to navigate life's deeper challenges wisely.

Nietzsche saw this crisis coming over a century ago. He warned that when education serves only economic utility, when universities become mere training grounds for careers rather than places for the cultivation of wisdom and character, we produce a culture of sophisticated barbarians—people with technical skills but no understanding of what those skills should serve.

Pierre Hadot, in his studies of ancient philosophy, reminds us what we have lost: "Philosophy was the love of and search for wisdom, and wisdom was, precisely, a certain way of life."

Philosophy is not about memorizing what dead philosophers said. It is about becoming a certain kind of person—one who can recognize truth, live virtuously, and act wisely. It is about transformation, not information. This is why the philosophical life cannot be pursued primarily for financial gain or career advancement.

Our culture has organized itself around accumulation—the gathering of things, credentials, information, power, and status. We often measure success by what we possess rather than the type of human being we actually *become*. The paradigm shift to valuing *being* over valuing possessions is much needed. This is not a new insight—it echoes through philosophy from the Stoics to the medievals, from Eastern traditions to modern existentialists. The good life is not found in what we accumulate but in who we become.

Remember Nietzsche's characterization: *"Careless, mocking, forceful—so does wisdom wish us: she is a woman, and never loves anyone but a warrior."* Wisdom demands courage because it requires facing truths we would rather avoid. It demands discipline because it develops only through sustained practice. It demands honesty because self-deception is wisdom's greatest enemy. The cultivation of wisdom is not optional—it is the most urgent task facing any individual who wishes to live well and any civilization that wishes to endure.

Plato ranked the highest virtues as Goodness, Truth, and Beauty. In a world filled with counterfeits—with false goods, comforting lies, and cheap pleasures masquerading as true beauty—how do we distinguish the genuine from the fake? Wisdom is that which allows us to recognize the Good, the True, and the Beautiful without falling for their imposters.

The ethos of any society—the underlying spirit of its culture; its attitude, its character, the virtues it values—determines its resilience. If we do not cultivate an ethos based on wisdom at the foundation, it is like building houses with no foundations and they will fail.

Hannah Arendt understood what is at stake: "Only people inspired by the Socratic eros, the love of wisdom, beauty, and justice, are capable of thought and can be trusted... The sad truth of the matter is that most evil is done by people who never made up their minds to be or do either evil or good."

But how do we develop this capacity to discern what truly matters? How do we overcome our blindness to our own biases and cultivate the judgment that wisdom requires? This is where we must turn to the most sophisticated way of thinking and communicating. This is where we must develop the proper spirit and utilize the dialectic process that we will discuss in the next chapter.

Philosophy is not a hobby, but a responsibility.

Again, it has been stated that "wisdom begins in wonder." I hope that you will have begun to wonder more about this concept of wisdom and that you will investigate it further:

Resources for further investigation:

- Plato, *Republic*

- Plato, *Symposium*

- Plato, *Apology*

- Pierre Hadot, *What Is Ancient Philosophy*

- Mortimer J. Adler, "Wisdom" (essay in *Great Books of the Western World*)

- Michel Ferrari and Nic M Weststrate, *The Scientific Study of Personal Wisdom*

- John Vervaeke and Christopher Mastropietro, *Awakening from the Meaning Crisis*

- Daniel Schmachtenberger, YouTube series *The War on Sensemaking* (5-part series from *Rebel Wisdom*)

CHAPTER 4

DIALECTIC OVER DEBATE

"What verse is for the poet, dialectical thinking is for the philosopher."

~Nietzsche, Philosophy in the Tragic Age of the Greeks

So, what is "dialectic," this thing that Plato referred to as "the coping-stone of the sciences" ranking it above all others and that Plotinus called "the precious part of philosophy"?

First, to be clear, when I use the term *dialectic*, I am referring to dialectic as it was formally introduced to the West through the dialogues of Plato. The word did not begin with Plato, but this was the most influential introduction in the context of philosophy and the weight of the word (in the Platonic tradition) means much more than superficial conversation. This is an important point because dialectic has often been redefined and used in different ways through more modern philosophy and therefore has often been misunderstood. For example, terms such as "Hegelian dialectic," "Marx's dialectical materialism," etc. We don't need to go into all of the details of every way it has been used in this case, but just understand that these are not the same thing, which is why "Hegelian" or "materialism" has been added to it, clearly signifying that this is something different from its original form. (In light of this, we should also be reminded of the point about things of value having a counterfeit).

The aim of the dialectic process is to bring one closer to Goodness, Truth, and Beauty—closer to wisdom. In short, you can begin to think of the concept of dialectic as the most sophisticated way of thinking and communicating. The more technically/scientifically appropriate definition would be as cognitive scientist John Vervaeke describes it: *A psychotechnology consisting of opponent processing + distributed cognition.*

Essentially, you can think of Platonic dialectic as the scientific method of philosophy. It also attempts to tackle issues that science is simply inadequate for, such as questions about love, justice, courage, wisdom, theology, etc. Just like the scientific method, *dialectic requires that one has the willingness and ability to try to disprove one's own preconceived notions*, which is not a way that we are naturally used to thinking and it takes much character building and training, which highlights again the vital importance of the subject of philosophy.

The Irreducible Nature of Dialectic

The concept of dialectic can also be frustrating and confusing for those first encountering it since it is another one of those words that resists a precise explanation. When people ask "What exactly is the dialectic method?" or "Give me the steps for doing dialectic," they are asking an impossible question—like asking "Tell me exactly how to paint a beautiful picture" or "Give me the precise steps for creating beautiful music."

These questions reveal a misunderstanding about the nature of dialectic itself. Dialectic is not a single methodology that can be packaged into a step-by-step instruction manual. It is a sophisticated way of thinking and communicating that involves utilizing multiple methodologies depending on the situation, the participants, and the subject matter at hand. Just as there is no single "method" for creating great art or music—no formula that, if followed precisely, will guarantee beautiful results—there is no single dialectical method that can be mechanically applied to every situation.

Consider the earlier example from Chapter 3 about wisdom and surfing: you cannot learn to surf a wave by reading about surfing technique, no matter how accurate or detailed the description. You must get in the water, you must feel the board beneath you, you must experience the motion of the wave, and you must fall many times before you develop the embodied knowledge of how to balance through a tube. No propositional knowledge—no matter how technically perfect—can substitute for this kind of participatory, embodied learning.

Dialectic works the same way. You cannot learn dialectical thinking by simply memorizing a set of rules or procedures. You must observe it. You must practice and participate in it.

Learning Through Observation and Practice

The dialectic process must be cultivated through observation of exemplars and through repeated engagement with the process itself.

This is why the Platonic dialogues remain indispensable after more than two millennia. They are not outdated textbooks containing information that has been superseded by more recent research. They are demonstrations of wisdom-seeking in action, and their value lies in showing us what dialectical thinking looks like when it's done well (and sometimes, when it's done poorly by Socrates' interlocutors who resist the process or when used improperly by the sophists).

This is likely why Plato wrote dialogues rather than treatises. The dialogues are not merely *about* dialectic—they *are* dialectic. They demonstrate the process in action. When you read the *Euthyphro*, you are not reading Plato's theory of piety presented in systematic form; you are watching the dialectic process unfold between Socrates and Euthyphro. You are observing how questions are asked, how assumptions are examined, how contradictions are revealed, how concepts are refined, how minds are opened (or sometimes, how they remain stubbornly closed).

You learn through the process: the conversational structure, the back-and-forth, the genuine uncertainty about where the conversation will lead, the moments of aporia (puzzlement/conflict), the occasional humor, the frustration, the insights that emerge not from one person lecturing but from two or more people thinking together.

Here is a crucial point that many miss when approaching Plato's dialogues:

If you dismiss the dialogues because you disagree with certain conclusions drawn, you are still in the shallow end of the pool and are missing the much deeper philosophical value. The value of studying the dialogues is not primarily in accepting or rejecting Socrates' conclusions about piety, justice, courage, or any other topic. The value lies in observing and learning the dialectic process itself—the most sophisticated way of thinking and communicating.

Again, philosophy is about *how* to think, not *what* to think. The dialogues teach us methods of inquiry, a way of examining beliefs, a process for collaborative truth-seeking. Whether you ultimately agree with the specific conclusions reached in any particular dialogue is almost beside the point. What matters is whether you can learn to think like a proper dialectician.

This is similar to how the scientific method functions. A scientist doesn't accept every scientific conclusion ever drawn as final truth. Science is self-correcting—as new evidence emerges, old theories are revised or replaced. But the scientific method itself—the process of forming hypotheses, testing them, examining evidence, drawing conclusions—remains valuable regardless of whether any particular scientific claim from the past still holds true today.

Dialectic works the same way. It is a self-correcting process. As new knowledge and insight are gained, conclusions can be revised, arguments can be refined, and understanding can deepen. The dialogues of Plato are not meant to be the final word on anything—they are meant to be the beginning of an ongoing conversation. The idea is for us to pick up where the dialogues conclude and continue the dialectic process, continue our journey of seeking wisdom.

Plato writes in the *Republic* (VII, 532-534):

> Dialectic, and dialectic alone, goes directly to the first principle and is the only science which does away with hypotheses in order to make her ground secure... And do you not call him a dialectician who is able to demand an account of the essence of each thing? And he who is unable to give an account of things either to himself or others, you would not call him intelligent?

Notice what Plato is emphasizing here: dialectic is concerned with seeking the essence of things, with examining foundations, with demanding coherent accounts. But he doesn't *give* us a formula for how to do this. Instead, throughout the dialogues, he *shows* us.

In the *Phaedrus* (276e-277a), Socrates makes this point explicitly when discussing the limitations of written texts:

> Writing shares a strange feature with painting. The offsprings of painting stand there as if they are alive, but if anyone asks them anything, they remain most solemnly silent. The same is true of written words. You'd think they were speaking as if they had some understanding, but if you question anything that has been said because you want to learn more, it continues to signify just that very same thing forever.

Socrates is warning us here: don't expect written philosophy to function like a technical manual. The written dialogues can show you dialectic in action and can inspire you to engage in dialectic yourself; but they cannot replace the living, ongoing exchange between minds. This is why philosophy must be practiced, not just studied.

Multiple Methodologies within Dialectic

Part of what makes dialectic difficult to explain is that skilled dialectical thinkers employ various approaches depending on what the situation requires. Sometimes dialectic involves:

- **Elenchus:** The method of cross-examination where one person asks questions to test another's beliefs for consistency

- **Division and Collection:** The process of carefully dividing concepts into natural kinds and then synthesizing them back together

- **Hypothesis Testing:** Proposing provisional explanations and examining their implications

- **Analogical Reasoning:** Using comparisons and metaphors to illuminate difficult concepts

- **Maieutics:** The "midwife" method of helping someone give birth to ideas they already possess but haven't articulated

- **Reductio ad Absurdum:** Following an opponent's reasoning to its logical conclusion to reveal hidden contradictions

A skilled dialectician knows when to employ each of these approaches, just as a skilled musician knows when to play softly and when to crescendo, when to maintain rhythm and when to syncopate. This judgment cannot be taught through rules alone—it develops through practice and experience.

Paradigm Shift Thinking

Imagine if we all approached our conversations with each other in the same way great musical artists approach making music together.

When great musical artists come together to collaborate, you can imagine all of the potential difficulties and dynamics involved, but when done properly the result of the collaboration is something much greater and more beautiful than could have ever been achieved individually. This process of collaboration is analogous to the dialectic process of great thinkers.

Vervaeke aptly makes this point:

> We are quite good at identifying biases in others, and we do so with remarkable ease. But when it comes to ourselves (our own distortions and self-deceptive patterns) we are terrible at it.
>
> And this tells us something crucial: You are my best source of self-correction, and I am yours.
>
> That insight goes to the very heart of what was meant to be the engine of democracy: A shared commitment to mutual correction in the service of truth and collective wisdom. But we've lost that.
>
> And to the extent that we withdraw into ourselves (becoming inwardly rigid or self-referential) we open the floodgates to self-deception.
>
> So the question naturally arises: How can we become aware of our self-deception?

This insight points to one of the fundamental problems of human cognition: we are remarkably blind to our own blind spots. We can often see clearly when others are being irrational, biased, or self-deceiving, but we have tremendous difficulty recognizing these same patterns in ourselves.

Our brains are not designed primarily to seek truth but to maintain consistency with our existing beliefs and to protect our sense of self. We naturally engage in what psychologists call "confirmation bias"—seeking out information that confirms what we already believe and avoiding or rationalizing away information that challenges our preconceptions. We are all walking around with a sophisticated "mental lawyer" whose job is not to find the truth but to make the strongest possible case for whatever we already want to believe. This is why our intelligence can become self-destructive.

The antidote to this issue is found in philosophy through the dialectic process.

A Jiu Jitsu Analogy

The term, "interlocutor" is used in Plato's dialogues. A general definition of "interlocutor" is simply somebody that is participating in a conversation. However, in terms of the dialectic process in the dialogues of Plato, this word should hold a little more weight. The beginning of the word is pronounced like "interlock," which is good way of thinking about it in the context of Plato's dialogues—two or more people intellectually "interlocking"—like two grapplers interlocking and about to wrestle.

First and foremost, it's important to understand that there is a non-negotiable prerequisite when it comes to proper participation in the dialectic process. This prerequisite is development of the proper spirit/character/attitude in order to participate in the dialectic process in the first place. We must prioritize the development of this proper spirit—the spirit of wonder, honesty and good faith. The willingness and ability to admit if/when we are wrong and to update our views when appropriate.

A perfect analogy to begin thinking about the proper dialectic spirit is sparring in the grappling martial art of jiu jitsu (or any martial art really). One of the first lessons that I had to learn when I began training in jiu jitsu is that when you're training/sparring with your partner you're typically not actually trying to "win" and you're certainly not trying to hurt your opponent; you're trying to learn and cooperate with your "opponent" in a way that is mutually beneficial. This is what John Vervaeke is referring to when he references *opponent processing + distributed cognition*. Through the "opponent processing" of sparring we are each learning from each other (distributed cognition).

What I observed early on was that the more skilled higher belts and those that were progressing at a higher pace would actually let themselves be put into bad and vulnerable positions so that they could practice and learn how to escape. Even though doing this may lead them to get submitted during a sparring session, they are taking in valuable information and improving their technique a little bit each time until they develop the knowledge and skills—or one might say *wisdom*—that will allow them to escape from worst-case scenarios and execute wisely at the proper time. Those were the people who were really advancing in their knowledge and skillset because they were constantly putting their *ideas* to the test. In the martial art of jiu jitsu your ideas get manifested into the physical world very quickly and very quickly you find out whether you had a good idea or a bad idea; sometimes in the form of being submitted, an injury or being choked unconscious. You can see that the character of those involved in the martial arts is vital. In order for learning to be maximized, one must involve partners who are trustworthy and operating in good faith. The same is true with interlocutors during the dialectic process.

This "opponent processing" and putting our ideas to the test are absolutely necessary for the processes of trying to figure out if we have good ideas or bad ideas relating to the world around us and to help us move closer to truth and wisdom. No reasonable person would ever imagine being able to improve their jiu jitsu skills to any semblance of proficiency without proper sparring experience. As the saying goes, "Like iron sharpens iron, so one man sharpens another." However, this simple and seemingly obvious lesson seems so often to be lost in the theoretical world and dealing with political or social issues. How many people actively avoid anything that may challenge or even destroy their preconceived notions and expose their bad ideas, rather than confronting and wrestling with the issues?

To emphasize again, the proper execution of this process is only possible when we develop our character and attitude first; prioritizing learning and truth and self-transformation over "winning." When we allow our desire to "win" an argument to overcome our desire to learn, we have lost the prerequisite dialectic spirit. Now, please don't misunderstand my overall point.

Nuance is always important. I am not saying there is *never* a time to try to win; there are jiu jitsu competitions or real-life self-defense situations and there are competition "debates" about various ideas in which the goal may appropriately be to win as a game; there is a time and place to make your case for why you have strong convictions about some issue that you find important. The point is that we cannot allow our want to "win" to come at the expense of truth and wisdom.

Dialectic vs. Debate: A Paradigm Shift

This also highlights an important point regarding the distinction between dialectic vs. debate. High schools and universities around the world have "debate clubs" and nearly everyone knows what it means to debate. It is essentially a competition like football, basketball, etc. with a perceived winner and a loser at the end. Teachers and professors of debate teams teach skills in rhetoric and tricks for influencing or manipulating people (sophistry), which in reality doesn't have any bearing on what may be right or true. Someone can "win" a debate (however that may be measured) and nobody involved may be any closer to the truth than when they began. In fact, if someone is skilled in rhetoric and other debate tactics, they can easily lie or deceive in various ways to actually lead people further away from the truth in the end.

Therefore, we need a better way for thinking and communicating and trying to make sense of our disagreements—better ways for truth seeking. This is where dialectic comes in. This is where the proper spirit/

attitude/character must be developed. This is where the paradigm shift in thinking must take place. Here is an example of "paradigm shift thinking" regarding this issue of debate vs. dialectic:

If I'm in a debate and the other person makes a valid point or presents compelling evidence that my argument is flawed and, in the end, I actually change my mind, I would be considered the "loser" of the debate. In contrast, if I'm properly participating in the true spirit of the dialectic process and someone makes a valid point or presents compelling evidence against my initial argument and I change my mind based on this new information, I would be considered honorable and I would be a "winner" in the true spirit of dialectic. I was the one that gained valuable new information; I was the one who became a little less ignorant and I am the one that can use my new knowledge to transform into a better human being.

Which attitude do you think is superior for communicating, making sense of the world, or seeking the truth and transforming oneself?

The answer here may seem obvious, but, in reality, it takes discipline and training of character development before one may even be able to recognize the truth when it goes against their preconceived notions or may be emotionally unsatisfying. Plato's dialogues propose that one aspect of thinking is often something like *remembering*. However, it is through the dialectic process that one is helped along the way to remember. This is why Socrates referred to himself as a metaphorical "midwife," helping his interlocutors to "give birth" to what was already inside of them.

If most of us think about it, we already know, somewhere in our conscious, that rather than "win" by deception, it's better to learn, to be *honorable*, to admit when one is wrong and adjust one's beliefs accordingly. But how many today actually *live* this (especially when it comes to contentious topics such as religion, politics, and social issues)? Sometimes we need a Socratic midwife, a formidable interlocutor, and some opponent processing to remind us what we really already knew.

Self-Transformation: The Little Deaths

In *The Book of Five Rings*, Musashi makes the point that "The warrior, however, understands that the end result of any study is a kind of death (sublime, not necessarily physical) before the attainment of perfection." Similarly, clinical psychologist Jordan Peterson advises "Every bit of learning is a little death. Every bit of new information challenges a previous conception, forcing it to dissolve into chaos before it can be reborn as something better. Sometimes such deaths virtually destroy us."

Human beings are instinctually geared toward survival, so welcoming this type of death does not come naturally and to do so takes much training, study, and discipline. Developing a proper balance of humility and ego is one key aspect of this character development that will allow us to open our minds and our souls to knowledge and wisdom that, like a metaphorical sword, will chop down at our current misconceptions about the universe and may cause the death of our current identity. It is this death that will lead us to the necessary self-transformation that can bring us at least a bit closer to some semblance of wisdom and a good life—something like a Phoenix rising from the ashes.

Some debate whether ego or humility is the most important characteristic of great warriors or wise men, but this debate is a trap. The choice between ego and humility is a false one. We simply want a humble ego; one that has been strengthened through humility. Proper humility will allow us to recognize our own ignorance and insufficiencies and will serve as the impetus for opening our minds and souls to the things that may destroy our false preconceived notions about the universe. However, it is the proper ego that will allow us to recognize that we have in us the potential, ability—and even the responsibility—for self-transformation through much training and study to become stronger, better, and wiser men.

> *So my soul was in rotten health. In an ulcerous condition it thrust itself to outward things, miserably avid to be scratched by contact with the world of the senses. Yet physical things had no soul. Love lay outside their range.*

This someone, whose "soul was in rotten health" eventually, through self-reflection and self-transformation, became known as Saint Augustine.

Human beings have the ability to make choices regarding their own self-transformations throughout life. Every time someone allows fear of the unknown and fearfulness of change overcome them and they avoid necessary self-transformation the world loses something of inestimable value.

> *If the caterpillar had the insight and ability to make a choice, but if it was scared of the unknown, hesitant and fearful of change, of self-transformation... how many fewer butterflies would the world be blessed with?*

The Danger of Isolation of Thought

Now I want to return to a previous point for reemphasis.

Think about how many people actively avoid legitimate information or evidence that may contradict their preconceived notions about any given topic, even in some extreme cases attempting to ban or censor certain speech that they don't like or with which they disagree. Throughout history there have always been those in positions of power who worked to shut down dissenting viewpoints in order to keep their positions of power to manipulate the masses. You can just take the stories of Socrates and Christ as two examples. This is a catastrophic decision because it literally stunts a society's ability to make sense of the world and think on a sophisticated level.

One resource to back this up is an essay by American economist, Thomas Sowell, aptly titled "The Tragedy of Isolation" (2013). In the essay, Sowell lays out compelling evidence regarding the history of detrimental effects that isolation has presented to cultures and societies around the world, specifically related to I.Q. Sowell discusses geographical isolation, cultural isolation due to government decisions, and self-imposed isolation by xenophobic cultures. Sowell's research illustrates the disastrous results for those isolated, including negative effects on I.Q, due to an inability or unwillingness to learn from others (think of the absence of the needed opponent processing and distributed cognition).

Jonathan Haidt is a moral psychologist and professor of ethical leadership at New York University's Stern School of Business who specializes in the psychology of morality and the moral emotions. Haidt is the author of *The Righteous Mind: Why Good People Are Divided by Politics and Religion,* in which one of the key findings from his extensive research regards the distinction between two kinds of cognition: intuition and reasoning. He points out that the moral emotions are a type of moral intuition.

Haidt concludes that humans are first and foremost ruled by intuition and emotion, not reasoning. Furthermore, the next step in the thought process is not to move to rationality, but to instinctually work to justify and reinforce what our initial feeling or intuition was. Haidt refers to this phenomenon as our "inner lawyer" at work. As a result, if our initial feeling or intuition about a subject is wrong, it is very difficult for us to correct flaws in our own thinking in order to bring us closer to the truth, rather than creating justifications for our wrong views. As Haidt points out, "We make our first judgments rapidly, and we are dreadful at seeking out evidence that might disconfirm those initial judgments. Yet friends can do for us what we cannot do for ourselves: they can challenge us, giving us reasons and arguments that sometimes trigger new intuitions, thereby making it possible for us to change our minds." Or as Carl Jung put it, "One almost always forgets or omits to apply to oneself the criticism that one hands out so freely to others, fascinated by the mote in one's brother's eye."

The point is that the antidote to all of this is the spirit and process of Platonic dialectic and the philosophical way of life.

The Relationship Between Philosophy and Theology: Two Pillars of Knowledge

I want to include some thoughts here about how dialectic can play a role in the relationship between philosophy and theology. I chose these two subjects because, again, they used to be considered two of the four pillars of knowledge, so I think it's important to bring them back into the dialectic process.

These two pillars of knowledge should not be in competition with each other; rather, they should be in dialectic with each other. When properly understood and implemented, there should be no conflict between philosophy and religion. In short and simple terms, whether conscious of the fact or not, human beings are religious by nature (we all worship something) and philosophy is necessary to help us *think* about and deal with that proposition. If the two seem to be in conflict with each other it is likely that our understanding of one or the other is insufficient or that we are dealing with a counterfeit of one or the other.

Only religion and philosophy properly *united* can offer the proper balance of the faith of religion with the humility and wonder of philosophy. Ideology is not all bad in and of itself; but it is that most precious part of philosophy, *dialectic*, that offers the antidote to the dragons of ideology. As Jordan Peterson makes the case in his book, *Maps of Meaning,* "Ideologies are powerful and dangerous." These powerful and dangerous ideologies can be used either for great evil or for righteousness; so it is important that we cultivate a culture built on a proper philosophical foundation with an emphasis on virtues and wisdom.

The spirit of dialectic is the bridge; the dialectic process is the utilization of that bridge to prevent one from becoming possessed by degenerate archetypes, dogmas, and ideologies. Dialectic offers the most sophisticated way to think about and navigate how we implement our faith, whatever it may be, into our everyday lives. Both will become unstable when either of these two pillars of knowledge are overlooked. And where both of these pillars of knowledge are removed, as in the West to a large degree, culture and society will inevitably begin to fail.

Friedrich Nietzsche's *Thus Spoke Zarathustra* is a brutal, unapologetic criticism of Christianity, which announced the metaphorical "death of God" in the West. It is understandable why Christians may see Nietzsche as a villain in the history of religion, but I propose that this would be a vital error. The dragons of ideology may guard and prevent one from studying and trying to understand Nietzsche's perspective in the context of his time, but *the spirit of dialectic* will make one *wonder* about what led Nietzsche to his conclusions and so many to the rejection of Christianity. I propose that the spirit of dialectic is the wise path. I'm afraid that if our culture begins to shift back toward religion and more religious traditions—forgive the cliché—if we don't study the mistakes of the past, we are doomed to repeat them once again.

Without philosophy religion loses its mind; without religion philosophy loses its soul.

However, that does not mean that I am reducing philosophy down to simply an intellectual endeavor. I'm just making the point that these two pillars of knowledge should work together as interlocutors participating in the dialectic process.

The Path Forward

If you want to develop dialectical capacity, here are some recommendations for where to begin:

1. **Develop the prerequisite character first:** *Cultivate intellectual humility, curiosity, courage, and honesty. Without these, technical proficiency in argument or the dialectic process becomes mere sophistry.*

2. **Read the dialogues:** *Start with accessible ones like Euthyphro, Crito, or Meno. Don't just read for content—watch how the conversations unfold.*

3. **Practice with others:** *Find people willing to engage in genuine philosophical conversation, where the goal is truth-seeking rather than winning.*

4. **Embrace discomfort:** *When you feel confused or when your beliefs are challenged, recognize this as a sign that genuine learning is happening.*

5. **Study exemplars:** *Beyond Plato, observe anyone who seems to think and communicate with wisdom—whether in person, in books, or in other media, particularly if they hold views in conflict with your own.*

6. **Reflect on your practice:** *After philosophical conversations, consider what went well and what didn't. Where did understanding deepen? Where did egos interfere? What could be done differently?*

Platonic dialectic is the bridge that allows us to cross from ignorance toward knowledge, from isolated thinking toward collaborative truth seeking, past the dragons of ideology toward the treasures of wisdom.

As Plato writes in the *Republic* (VII, 540a-b):

> Those who have come this far must be compelled to lift up the radiant light of their souls to what itself provides light for everything... Then, when they have seen the good itself, they must each in turn put the city and its citizens and themselves in order, using it as their model.

The dialectical journey is ultimately about transformation—not just learning new information, but becoming the kind of person who can see clearly, think wisely, and act righteously. That transformation, like all profound human development, cannot be reduced to a set of instructions. It must be lived.

There is no more important question to ask when considering one's own beliefs than, "How would I find out if I were wrong?" There also may be no question more dangerous—dangerous for the ego, dangerous for your world view, dangerous to your relationships, dangerous because people may turn against you and you may make enemies. It can be dangerous in that you may actually become convinced that a wrong perspective is right.

You can easily see where courage and wisdom must be part of this equation and I propose that it would be much more dangerous not to ask the question in the first place.

To further investigate these matters:

- Plato, *Meno*

- Plato, *Phaedrus*

- Plato, *Theaetetus*

- John Vervaeke, (YouTube series) *After Socrates*

- Plotinus, *The First Ennead*

- Francisco J. Gonzalez, *Dialectic and Dialogue: Plato's Practice of Philosophical Inquiry*

- Jens Kristian Larsen, Vivil Valvik Haraldsen, and Justin Vlasits, *New Perspectives on Platonic Dialectic: A Philosophy of Inquiry*

CHAPTER 5

WHAT IS REALLY ON THE LINE

"Do but despise intellect and knowledge, the highest of all man's gifts, and thou hast surrendered thyself to the devil and to perdition art doomed." ~ Goethe, Faust

I'll begin this chapter with an emphasis on metaphor, because I will use metaphor heavily in this final chapter. Moral psychologist Jonathan Haidt has asserted, "Human thinking depends on metaphor. We understand new or complex things in relation to things we already know." Haidt adds, "Our life is the creation of our minds, and we do much of that creating with metaphor. We see new things in terms of things we already understand.... With the wrong metaphor we are deluded; with no metaphor we are blind." Aristotle has previously proclaimed "The greatest thing by far is to be a master of metaphor; it is the one thing that cannot be learned from others; and it is also a sign of genius, since a good metaphor implies an intuitive perception of the similarity of the dissimilar."

The power of metaphor lies in its ability to make the abstract concrete, the distant immediate, the complex simple. When Goethe speaks of surrendering to "the devil," he may not necessarily be making a literal theological claim but using a powerful metaphor to describe what happens when human beings abandon their highest capacity—the ability to think, learn, and grow in wisdom. The "devil" represents whatever forces in the world and in ourselves that would keep us ignorant, passive, and spiritually impoverished.

You don't need to dwell on the metaphysical to extrapolate Goethe's powerful metaphorical warning and how it relates to our own individual lives, as well as all of civilization. The world is certainly filled with beauty, but there is no denying that life is also filled with suffering; both inevitable and unnecessary suffering. Knowledge and particularly wisdom can help us mitigate that suffering. Not only can they help us avoid unnecessary suffering, but knowledge and wisdom can also help us better handle ourselves and better navigate the inevitable suffering that every human being will encounter over their lifetime. The aim of this powerful metaphor by Goethe was to bring to light that truth, that when you forego the pursuit of knowledge and intellect—of wisdom, you are voluntarily surrendering yourself to unnecessary suffering. A fact of life that too few ever consider is given by clinical psychologist Jordan Peterson: *"If your life isn't going well, perhaps it is your current knowledge that is insufficient, not life itself."*

This insight turns the common narrative of victimhood on its head. Rather than assuming that life is simply unfair or that we are passive victims of circumstances beyond our control, this suggests that much of our suffering may be due to our own ignorance and lack of wisdom—ignorance that could, in principle, be remedied through learning and growth–through seeking wisdom and self-transformation.

Furthermore, do not make the mistake of thinking that the consequences of one's suffering are limited to the individual alone, as the actions of an individual will always have at least some effect on the people and the world around the individual and far beyond what one may imagine. As is aptly articulated by Thomas Hobbes in the *Leviathan*: "There is no action of man in this life that is not the beginning of so long a chain of consequences as no human providence is high enough to give a man a prospect to the end."

The words and actions of the individual travel far beyond what we can ever imagine. Our words and our actions are that powerful. We do not get to decide whether or not we will have an impact on the world and those around us, only some degree of what that impact may be. I assert that the best way through life is to accept that great responsibility and rise to the occasion through the acquisition of and the passing along of knowledge and wisdom. I assert that there is no more noble cause for mankind than this. When you influence just one person (positively or negatively) ... well, you *never* just influence just one person. If the world could use more human beings with courage, strength and wisdom – it starts with the individual.

In all great works of fiction there is always some profound, underlying "truth." These two excerpts from the great novel *The Brothers Karamazov* by Fyodor Dostoevsky serve as not just a lesson, but a warning of the profound impact that the individual has on the world around them and far beyond. Echoing the sentiments of the previous Thomas Hobbes quote, this is a warning articulated as only Dostoevsky could and it's worth serious reflection. We can all do better:

> Every day and every hour, every minute, walk round yourself and watch yourself, and see that your image is a seemly one. You pass by a little child, you pass by, spiteful, with ugly words, with wrathful heart; you may not have noticed the child, but he has seen you, and your image, unseemly and ignoble, may remain in his defenseless heart. You don't know it, but you may have sown an evil seed in him and it may grow, and all because you were not careful before the child, because you did not foster in yourself a careful, actively benevolent love.

> My brother asked the birds to forgive him; that sounds senseless, but it is right; for all is like an ocean, all is flowing and blending; a touch in one place sets up movement at the other end of the earth. It may be senseless to beg forgiveness of the birds, but birds would be happier at your side—a little happier, anyway—and children

and all animals, if you were nobler than you are now. It's all like an ocean, I tell you.

Dostoevsky's vision of reality as an "ocean" where "a touch in one place sets up movement at the other end of the earth" provides a poetic expression of what modern science confirms: we live in a system of incredible interconnectedness where small actions can have large and unpredictable consequences.

The Nature of Evil and Ignorance

This won't be an exhaustive point about the nature of evil, but it's been written that Socrates asserted long ago that ignorance is the cause of much more suffering than evil intentions. That is not to say that everyone who is ignorant of something is evil (that would obviously include every human being), although, here it is worth heeding the words of Alexander Solzhenitsyn from *The Gulag Archipelago*:

> The line separating good and evil passes not through states, nor between classes, nor between political parties either—but right through every human heart—and through all human hearts. This line shifts. Inside us, it oscillates with the years. And even within hearts overwhelmed by evil, one small bridgehead of good is retained.

Furthermore, Solzhenitsyn expresses:

> If only there were evil people somewhere insidiously committing evil deeds, and it were

necessary only to separate them from the rest of us and destroy them. But the line dividing good and evil cuts through the heart of every human being. And who is willing to destroy a piece of his own heart?

Although some capacity for evil is present in each individual, most evil is not committed by those who know or believe that they are evil or committing evil acts. As Jordan Peterson has described it, "Evil is the process by which the significance of the anomaly is denied; the process by which meaning itself—truth itself—is rejected." Haidt explains, "Moral motivations (justice, honor, loyalty, patriotism) enter into most acts of violence, including terrorism and war. Most people believe their actions are morally justified." Likewise, Hannah Arendt in *The Life of the Mind* argues

> Where does this leave us in regard to one of our chief problems—the possible interconnectedness of non-thought and evil? We are left with the conclusion that only people inspired by the Socratic eros, the love of wisdom, beauty, and justice, are capable of thought and can be trusted. In other words, we are left with Plato's 'noble natures,' with the few of whom it may be true that none does evil voluntarily.

> Yet the implied and dangerous conclusion, 'Everybody wants to be good' is not true even in their case. (The sad truth of the matter is that most evil is done by people who never made up their minds to be or do either evil or good.)

Peterson's definition of evil as "the process by which the significance of the anomaly is denied" points to something crucial: evil often involves not the embrace of falsehood but the rejection of truth. When we encounter information that challenges our comfortable assumptions, that suggests we might need to change our behavior or admit we were wrong, we face a choice. We can engage with this information honestly, allowing it to transform us if necessary. Or we can deny its significance, dismiss it as irrelevant, rationalize it away.

This is why Arendt concludes that only those inspired by "Socratic eros"—the love of wisdom, beauty, and justice—can be truly trusted. Only those who have made a fundamental commitment to truth over comfort, to growth over stagnation, to reality over illusion, have the internal resources necessary to resist the temptations that lead ordinary people to participate in evil.

The Path Forward

These are invaluable lessons and thoughts to consider, referencing some of the greatest thinkers throughout history. Again, we don't get to choose if we will have an impact, we only have some degree of control of what that impact may be. I assert that if we feel any sense of responsibility at all to have a positive impact for ourselves, our loved ones, civilization and the entire world around us, the most prudent and noble that one can strive for is the acquisition of and the passing along of knowledge and wisdom. As is so aptly said in the following quote by Adam Rose, referencing American philosopher Robert Hutchins, who was President and

Chancellor of the University of Chicago, regarding liberal arts education (philosophy being the cornerstone of the liberal arts).

> Hutchins concluded that the liberal arts are not merely indispensable; they are unavoidable. Nobody can decide for himself whether he is going to be a human being, the only question open to him is whether he will be an ignorant undeveloped one or one who has sought to reach the highest point he is capable of attaining. The question in short is whether he will be a poor liberal artist or a good one.

Hutchins' observation cuts to the heart of human dignity and responsibility. We do not get to choose whether we will be human beings—that is given. But we do get to choose what kind of human beings we will be.

Friedrich Nietzsche famously said, "He who has a why to live, can bear almost any how." If one does not fully grasp the consequences and the deep meaning (the why) when it comes to the significance of the acquisition of knowledge and seeking wisdom beyond the superficial level (getting a good paying job, learning a new hobby, etc.), one will likely never bother, let alone strive to be successful with the subsequent "how," beyond the very basic and superficial. It will require much sacrifice and the noble quest for wisdom is certainly not for the faint of heart. Jordan Peterson has said: "Every bit of learning is a little death. Every bit of new information challenges a previous conception, forcing it to dissolve into chaos before it can be reborn as something better. Sometimes such deaths virtually destroy us."

Understanding the "why" of philosophical education is crucial because the path is genuinely difficult. It requires giving up comfortable illusions, confronting uncomfortable truths about ourselves and our world, and taking on responsibilities that many people prefer to avoid.

A long, difficult and even dangerous journey lies ahead for the genuine truth seeker—Socrates and many others have lost their lives along the way, although as Socrates proclaims in the *Apology*:

> Someone will say: And are you not ashamed, Socrates, of a course of life which is likely to bring you to an untimely end? To him I may fairly answer: There you are mistaken: a man who is good for anything ought not to calculate the chance of living or dying; he ought only to consider whether in doing anything he is doing right or wrong—acting the part of a good man or of a bad one. [28]

My hope is that by now I have made the why clear enough to naturally manifest the motivation, inspiration and discipline to overcome the challenges regarding the how. You must voluntarily confront and slay the metaphorical dragons in order to acquire the treasures of life.

The metaphor of slaying dragons to acquire treasure captures something essential about the philosophical journey. The dragons represent everything within ourselves and in our culture and the world that resists wisdom: our laziness, our pride, our fear of change, our attachment to comfortable illusions, our desire for easy answers to difficult questions.

> You, my friend,— a citizen of the great and mighty and wise city of Athens,—are you not ashamed of heaping up the greatest amount of money and honour and reputation, and caring so little about wisdom and truth and the greatest improvement of the soul, which you never regard or heed at all?—Socrates, *Apology* [29]

CONCLUSION

This book began with a simple but profound claim: that philosophy is the most important subject because it is the subject that shapes the way we approach and think about every other subject. We have seen how this claim unfolds across multiple dimensions of human existence.

We have explored what it means to be an ordinary person called to extraordinary service, how the greatest achievements in human history have come not from those born with special advantages but from those who were willing to develop their character and capabilities.

We have examined what philosophy truly is: not an academic exercise or intellectual game, but the love of wisdom that transforms both the lover and the beloved. We have seen how this love requires both intellectual humility and moral courage, both openness to truth and commitment to growth. Wisdom involves action— one must act wisely.

We have investigated the art of dialectical thinking, the most sophisticated method available for overcoming our natural tendencies toward bias, self-deception, self-destruction and intellectual isolation. We have learned how genuine dialogue with others who challenge our assumptions is essential for rational thought and moral development.

Finally, we have grasped what is really at stake in all of this: not just our own sense of inner peace, but the wellbeing of everyone whose life we touch, the health of our communities and institutions, potentially the future of human civilization itself.

The philosophical life is not easy, but it is necessary. It is not comfortable, but it is rewarding. It is not for everyone, but it is available to everyone who has the courage to begin the journey. Evil is a spirit that is always lurking and only needs the help of passivity and weak men to propagate. The invitation is extended to you—will you help reignite the love of wisdom?

"The ideal man is a philosopher, artist, and warrior."~Benvenuto Cellini

FURTHER QUOTATIONS FOR CONTEMPLATION

*"A good person fights temptation;
a wise person learns to be tempted by
the good."*

~Vervaeke and L. Ferraro

*"What then is that which is able to
conduct a man? One thing and only
one, philosophy."*

~Marcus Aurelius

*"Wise, I may not call them; for that is a
great name which belongs to God alone,
—lovers of wisdom or philosophers is
their modest and befitting title."*

~Socrates

"I've already lost touch with a couple of people I used to be."

~Joan Didion

"If philosophical theories seduce you, sit down and go over them again and again in your mind. But never call yourself a philosopher, and never allow yourself to be called a philosopher."

~Epictetus

"I think there is no one who has rendered worse service to the human race than those who have learned philosophy as a mercenary trade."

~Seneca

"Sophists hunt the rich and young; philosophers are impartial and friendly to all."

~Xenophon

"What is the first business of him who philosophizes? To throw away self-conceit. For it is impossible for a man to begin to learn that which he thinks that he knows."

~Epictetus